IRELAND T

The Ultimate Guide to Discovering the Best Places to Visit, Things to Do, and Must-Try Irish Experiences.

(Essential Travel Guide)

By Walden Caldwell

Table of Contents

My First Visit to Ireland

My first visit to Ireland was a dream come true. As a lover of history and culture, I had always wanted to explore the Emerald Isle and see its famous landmarks for myself. I was not disappointed.

I landed in Dublin, the capital city of Ireland, and immediately felt the energy of the city. The streets were bustling with people, the pubs were lively, and the architecture was stunning. I checked into my hotel and set out to explore.

My first stop was Trinity College, where I saw the famous Book of Kells. The intricate illustrations and calligraphy of this ancient manuscript left me in awe. I also visited the Old Library, which houses the Long Room, a beautiful chamber filled with thousands of ancient books. It was a bibliophile's paradise.

From Trinity College, I walked to St. Patrick's Cathedral, the largest church in Ireland. The Gothic architecture and impressive size of the cathedral left me in awe. Inside, I was struck by the intricate carvings and stained glass windows. I sat in silence for a while, taking in the beauty and history of the place.

After my visit to the cathedral, I decided to explore the city on foot. I walked through the streets of Dublin, taking in the colorful buildings and the lively atmosphere. I stopped to grab a pint at a traditional Irish pub and listened to live music. It was a great way to experience the local culture.

The next day, I took a train to the Cliffs of Moher, one of the most famous landmarks in Ireland. The cliffs rise 700 feet above the Atlantic Ocean and offer breathtaking views of the coast. As I walked along the edge, I felt the wind in my hair and the spray of the sea on my face. The scenery was truly breathtaking.

After my visit to the cliffs, I took a bus to the small town of Galway. The town is known for its traditional Irish music, and I was not disappointed. I spent my evening listening to live music in a cozy pub, surrounded by locals and tourists alike. It was a great way to end my day.

The next day, I took a day trip to the Ring of Kerry, a scenic drive along the coast of

Ireland. I was struck by the beauty of the landscapes, from the rugged cliffs to the lush green hills. I stopped at a number of small villages along the way, where I got a chance to see traditional Irish life up close.

On my last day, I returned to Dublin and visited the Guinness Storehouse, the home of the famous Irish stout. I learned about the history of the brewery and the process of making Guinness. I also got to taste a pint of Guinness at the Gravity Bar, which offers panoramic views of the city.

My first visit to Ireland was an unforgettable experience. I was struck by the country's rich history and culture, and by the warmth and hospitality of the people. I can't wait to go back and explore more of this beautiful country.

Chapter 1: Introduction to Ireland

Ireland, also known as the Emerald Isle, is a small island nation located in northwestern Europe. Known for its lush green landscapes, vibrant culture, and friendly people, Ireland is a popular destination for tourists from around the world. Whether you're interested in history, culture, outdoor activities, or just a good pint of Guinness, Ireland has something for everyone.

One of the main draws of Ireland is its stunning natural beauty. The country is home to a diverse range of landscapes, from the rugged cliffs of the Wild Atlantic Way to the rolling green hills of the Wicklow Mountains. Visitors can hike through the countryside, explore coastal paths, or simply take in the stunning views from a local pub or restaurant.

Another important aspect of Irish culture is its rich history and heritage. Visitors can explore ancient ruins and castles, such as the rock of Cashel, Kilkenny Castle and many more. The country is also home to many important historical sites, including the Hill of Tara, which was the ancient seat of the High Kings of Ireland, and the Cliffs of Moher, which have been a popular tourist destination for centuries.

Ireland is also known for its vibrant culture, which is reflected in its music, dance, and literature. Visitors can experience traditional Irish music at local pubs and festivals, or take in a traditional Irish dance performance. The country is also home to many famous writers and poets, including W.B. Yeats, James Joyce, and Samuel Beckett.

One of the best ways to experience Irish culture is by visiting one of the many local markets and festivals that take place throughout the country. These events are a great opportunity to sample local food and drink, listen to live music, and meet local people. Some of the most popular festivals include the Galway Arts Festival, the Cork Jazz Festival, and the Dublin Writers Festival.

When it comes to food, Ireland is famous for its hearty and comforting cuisine. Visitors can sample traditional Irish dishes such as Irish stew, colcannon, and soda bread. The country is also known for its seafood, particularly its wild Atlantic salmon and oysters. And of course, no trip to Ireland would be complete without trying a pint of Guinness, the country's most famous export.

Ireland is also a great destination for outdoor activities. Visitors can go hiking, horseback riding, fishing, and many more outdoor activities. The country is also home to many world-class golf courses, including the famous Ballybunion Golf Club, which is considered one of the best golf courses in the world.

When it comes to accommodations, Ireland offers a wide range of options, from budget-friendly hostels and bed and breakfasts to luxury hotels and resorts. Visitors can choose to stay in the heart of the city or in the countryside, depending on their preferences.

In conclusion, Ireland is a small but mighty country with a lot to offer visitors. Whether you're interested in history, culture, or outdoor activities, Ireland has something for everyone. With its stunning landscapes, vibrant culture, and friendly people, Ireland is a destination that should not be missed.

Overview of Ireland's History and Culture

Ireland has a rich and complex history, dating back to prehistoric times. The island has been inhabited for over 9,000 years and has been shaped by a variety of cultures and influences. From the ancient Celts and

Vikings to the Normans and English, Ireland has a diverse and fascinating past.

One of the earliest civilizations in Ireland was the Celts, who arrived on the island around the 4th century BC. They were a powerful and influential culture, known for their art, metalworking, and religious practices. They also developed an oral tradition of storytelling, which continues to be a vital part of Irish culture to this day.

The Vikings arrived in Ireland in the 8th century AD, and they had a significant impact on the island. They established settlements and trading centers, such as Dublin and Waterford, and their influence can still be seen in the form of place names, language and customs.

In the 12th century, the Normans arrived in Ireland and established a powerful presence on the island. They built castles and forts, such as Trim Castle and Dublin Castle, and their influence can still be seen in the architecture and culture of Ireland today.

The English arrived in Ireland in the 16th century, and their relationship with the Irish people was often fraught with conflict. The English imposed their laws, language, and religion on the Irish people, and this led to centuries of resistance and rebellion. The most famous of these was the Easter Rising of 1916, which marked the beginning of the Irish War of Independence.

The Irish War of Independence officially ended in 1922, with the signing of the Anglo-Irish Treaty, which established the Irish Free State. This was followed by the Irish Civil War, which lasted until 1923. In 1949, Ireland officially became a republic, and it has been an independent nation ever since.

Ireland's culture is deeply rooted in its history and heritage. The Irish people are proud of their heritage and are known for their love of storytelling, music, dance, and literature. The traditional Irish music is an important aspect of the culture and it is often played in the pubs, festivals and events. The most famous traditional Irish dance is the Irish step dance, which is known for its rapid footwork and intricate moves.

The Irish people are also known for their love of literature, and the country has produced many famous writers, including W.B. Yeats, James Joyce, and Samuel Beckett. The literature in Ireland has been an important part of the culture for centuries, and it reflects the country's history, heritage, and identity.

The Irish culture is also reflected in its art, architecture, and crafts. Visitors can admire the intricate metalwork, colorful stained glass, and intricate stone carvings found in many of Ireland's historic buildings. The traditional Irish crafts, such as knitting, pottery, and weaving, are also an important part of the culture and can be found in many of the local markets and shops.

In conclusion, Ireland has a rich and complex history that has shaped the country's culture and identity. From the ancient Celts and Vikings to the Normans and English, Ireland has been influenced by a variety of cultures and civilizations. Today, the Irish people are proud of their heritage and continue to celebrate it through music, dance, literature, art, and crafts. The country's culture and history are an integral part of what makes Ireland such a unique and fascinating destination for visitors.

Geography and Climate

Ireland is an island nation located in northwestern Europe, and it is the third-largest island in Europe and the twentieth-largest island in the world. The island is divided into two political entities: the Republic of Ireland, which covers most of the island, and Northern Ireland, which is part of the United Kingdom. The island is surrounded by the Atlantic Ocean, the Irish Sea, and the Celtic Sea.

The geography of Ireland is diverse, ranging from rugged cliffs and rocky shores to rolling hills and lush green landscapes. The west coast of Ireland is characterized by the Wild Atlantic Way, a scenic coastal route that takes in some of the most spectacular landscapes in the country, including the Cliffs of Moher, the Aran Islands, and the Ring of Kerry. The east coast is characterized by the rolling hills of Wicklow and the gentle landscapes of the Irish Midlands. The central part of the island is characterized by the River Shannon, the longest river in Ireland, and the surrounding lakes and wetlands.

The climate of Ireland is classified as a temperate maritime climate, which means that it is mild and wet. The country experiences cool summers and mild winters, with temperatures rarely dropping below freezing. The average temperature in Ireland ranges from 7 to 12 degrees Celsius (45 to 54 degrees Fahrenheit) throughout the year. Rainfall is fairly consistent throughout the year, with the wettest months being October and November. The average annual rainfall is between 800 and 1,200 millimeters (31 and 47 inches).

The west coast of Ireland is known for its high rainfall, with the areas around the Cliffs of Moher and the Ring of Kerry experiencing some of the highest levels in the country. The east coast is generally drier, with the Wicklow Mountains and the Irish Midlands experiencing lower levels of rainfall.

Ireland is also known for its strong winds, particularly on the west coast. The winds can be strong enough to cause damage to buildings and vehicles, and they can make outdoor activities such as hiking and cycling challenging.

In conclusion, Ireland's geography and climate are diverse and varied, with a range of landscapes, from rugged cliffs to rolling hills, and a mild and wet climate. The west coast is known for its high rainfall and strong winds, while the east coast is generally drier. The country's unique climate and geography make it a destination that offers visitors a wide range of outdoor activities and attractions, from hiking and cycling to enjoying the natural beauty of the landscape.

Tips on language, currency, and customs

When traveling to Ireland, it is important to be familiar with the local language, currency, and customs. The official language of Ireland is English, however, many people also speak Irish, which is also known as Gaelic. Irish is a Celtic language and it is considered an official language of the country. It is spoken primarily in the western and southern regions of the country, particularly in rural areas. Although not everyone in Ireland speaks Irish, many road signs, public notices, and official documents are written in both English and Irish.

The currency used in Ireland is the Euro (EUR). ATMs and currency exchange facilities are widely available throughout the country, and most major credit cards are accepted in shops, restaurants, and hotels. Tipping is not expected in Ireland, however, it is common to leave a small amount of money (10-15%) in restaurants and cafes if you are happy with the service.

When it comes to customs, Ireland is a relatively informal country, and visitors should not feel the need to dress up. However, it is important to be respectful of local customs and traditions. Ireland is a predominantly Catholic country and it is important to be mindful of religious holidays and events. For example, it is customary to remove hats and caps when entering a church or other religious building.

In Ireland, it is considered impolite to speak loudly or to shout in public, and visitors should avoid using profanity in public. The Irish people are known for their warmth and hospitality, and visitors should be respectful of local customs and traditions.

When it comes to drinking, it is important to note that the legal drinking age in Ireland is 18. Drinking in public is not prohibited, but it is not recommended to drink excessively in public places. It is also important to note that Ireland has strict laws regarding drinking and driving, and visitors should be aware of the legal limit.

In conclusion, Ireland is a welcoming and friendly country with a rich culture and history. Visitors should be familiar with the local language, currency, and customs to ensure a smooth and enjoyable trip. The official language is English, but many people also speak Irish. The currency used is the Euro and it is important to note that the legal drinking age is 18. The Irish culture is relatively informal, but visitors should be respectful of local customs and traditions. Being mindful of these tips will help visitors to understand the country better and to have a great experience.

Chapter 2: Accommodations

When it comes to accommodations in Ireland, there are a variety of options available to suit different budgets and preferences. From luxury hotels to budget-friendly hostels, there is something for everyone.

For luxury accommodations, Ireland offers a wide range of five-star hotels, such as the Ashford Castle and the Adare Manor. These hotels offer luxurious amenities, such as spa facilities, fine dining restaurants, and beautiful grounds. Visitors can also choose to stay in a traditional Irish castle, such as the Dromoland Castle or the Ashford Castle, which offer a unique and authentic experience.

For mid-range accommodations, visitors can choose from a variety of three- and four-star hotels, guesthouses, and B&Bs. These options offer comfortable accommodations at a more affordable price point, and they are often located in charming and picturesque locations. Many of these accommodations also offer traditional Irish breakfast, which is a must-try experience.

For budget-friendly options, visitors can choose from a variety of hostels, camping and caravan sites, and budget hotels. These accommodations offer basic amenities at a lower price point, and they are often located in convenient locations. Hostels in Ireland are known for their friendly atmosphere, and they often offer a variety of facilities and activities, such as shared kitchens and lounges, which provide an opportunity to meet other travelers.

Another option for accommodations in Ireland is vacation rentals, which include apartments, cottages, and houses. These options offer more space and privacy than traditional hotel accommodations and can be a good option for families or groups of friends.

When choosing accommodations in Ireland, it is important to consider the location, amenities, and price. It is also recommended to research the accommodations before booking, to ensure that the accommodation you choose meets your needs and preferences.

In conclusion, Ireland offers a wide range of accommodations options for visitors, from luxury hotels to budget-friendly hostels. Visitors can choose from five-star hotels, traditional Irish castles, mid-range hotels, guesthouses, B&Bs, hostels, camping and caravan sites, budget hotels and vacation rentals. It is important to consider the location, amenities, and price when choosing accommodations and to research the options before booking. With the right accommodations, visitors can enjoy a comfortable and memorable stay in Ireland.

Options for hotels, hostels, guesthouses, and rental properties in Ireland

When it comes to choosing accommodations in Ireland, there are a variety of options available to suit different budgets and preferences. Here is an overview of the different types of accommodations available in Ireland:

Hotels: Ireland offers a wide range of hotels, from luxury five-star options to budget-friendly three-star options. Luxury hotels in Ireland, such as the Ashford Castle and the Adare Manor, offer luxurious amenities, such as spa facilities, fine dining restaurants, and beautiful grounds. Mid-range hotels, such as the Kilkenny Ormonde Hotel and the Galway Bay Hotel, offer comfortable accommodations at a more affordable price point, often in charming and picturesque locations. Budget hotels, such as the Ibis Dublin and the Travelodge Dublin, offer basic amenities at a lower price point, and they are often located in convenient locations.

Hostels: Hostels in Ireland offer budget-friendly accommodations for travelers. They often have shared dormitory-style rooms, as well as private rooms. Hostels in Ireland are known for their friendly atmosphere, and they often offer a variety of facilities and activities, such as shared kitchens and lounges, which provide an opportunity to meet other travelers. Popular hostels in Ireland include the Generator Hostel Dublin, the Kinlay House Dublin, and the Kinlay House Cork.

Guesthouses: Guesthouses in Ireland offer a more homely and intimate experience than hotels. They often have a family-run atmosphere and they are known for their traditional Irish breakfast. Some guesthouses also have self-catering facilities. Guesthouses in Ireland can be found in charming and picturesque locations, such as the countryside or small towns. Popular guesthouses in Ireland include the Blarney Woollen Mills Guesthouse and the Killarney Guesthouse.

Vacation Rentals: Vacation rentals in Ireland include apartments, cottages, and houses. These options offer more space and privacy than traditional hotel accommodations and can be a good option for families or groups of friends. They often have self-catering facilities and they can be found in a variety of locations, such as the countryside, small towns, and cities. Popular vacation rental options in Ireland include the Irish Cottage Rentals and the Irish Country Cottages.

When it comes to choosing accommodations in Ireland, it's important to consider the location, amenities, and price. It's also recommended to research the accommodations before booking to ensure that the accommodation you choose meets your needs and preferences.

In conclusion, Ireland offers a wide range of accommodations options for visitors, from luxury hotels to budget-friendly hostels, guesthouses and vacation rentals. Visitors can choose from five-star hotels, mid-range hotels, guesthouses, hostels and vacation rentals. It is important to consider the location, amenities, and price when choosing accommodations and to research the options before booking. With the right accommodations, visitors can enjoy a comfortable and memorable stay in Ireland.

Recommendations for budget, mid-range, and luxury accommodations in different parts of the country

Ireland offers a wide range of accommodations options for visitors, and the country can be divided into several regions, each with its own unique attractions and accommodations options.

Here are some recommendations for budget, mid-range, and luxury accommodations in different parts of the country:

Dublin:

- Budget: The Generator Hostel Dublin is a popular budget option in the heart of the city, offering dormitory-style rooms as well as private rooms.
- Mid-range: The Kilkenny Ormonde Hotel is a great mid-range option in the city center, offering comfortable accommodations with a variety of amenities.
- Luxury: The Westbury Hotel is a luxurious option located in the heart of Dublin, offering elegant accommodations and a variety of amenities including a spa and fitness center.

Galway:

- Budget: The Kinlay House Galway is a budget-friendly option located in the city center, offering dormitory-style rooms as well as private rooms.
- Mid-range: The Galway Bay Hotel is a great mid-range option located on the waterfront, offering comfortable accommodations and great views of Galway Bay.
- Luxury: The g Hotel & Spa is a luxurious option located in the city center, offering elegant accommodations and a variety of amenities including a spa and fitness center.

Killarney:

- Budget: The Killarney International Hostel is a budget-friendly option located in the city center, offering dormitory-style rooms as well as private rooms.
- Mid-range: The Killarney Guesthouse is a great mid-range option located in

the city center, offering comfortable accommodations and traditional Irish breakfast.

- Luxury: The Dunloe Hotel & Gardens is a luxurious option located in the countryside, offering elegant accommodations and beautiful gardens.

Cork:

- Budget: The Kinlay House Cork is a budget-friendly option located in the city center, offering dormitory-style rooms as well as private rooms.
- Mid-range: The Cork International Hotel is a great mid-range option located in the city center, offering comfortable accommodations and a variety of amenities.
- Luxury: The Hayfield Manor is a luxurious option located in the city center, offering elegant accommodations and a variety of

amenities including a spa and fitness center.

Cliffs of Moher:

- Budget: The Doolin Hostel is a budget-friendly option located in the village of Doolin, offering dormitory-style rooms as well as private rooms.
- Mid-range: The Armada Hotel is a great mid-range option located in the village of Spanish Point, offering comfortable accommodations and great views of the Cliffs of Moher.
- Luxury: The Bellbridge House Hotel is a luxurious option located in the village of Spanish Point, offering elegant accommodations and a variety of amenities including a spa and fitness center.

In conclusion, Ireland offers a wide range of accommodations options for visitors, from budget-friendly hostels and guesthouses to luxurious hotels, in various parts of the country. Whether you're looking for a budget-friendly option in Dublin, a mid-range option in Galway, or a luxurious option in Killarney, there is something for everyone in Ireland. It's important to research the accommodations before booking to ensure that the accommodation you choose meets your needs and preferences and to consider the location, amenities and price. With the right accommodations, visitors can enjoy a comfortable and memorable stay in Ireland.

Information on amenities and services offered by each type of accommodation

When choosing accommodations in Ireland, it's important to consider the amenities and services that are important to you. Here is an overview of the amenities and services offered by the different types of accommodations in Ireland:

Hotels:

- Luxury hotels in Ireland typically offer a wide range of amenities, such as spa facilities, fitness centers, fine dining restaurants, and beautiful grounds.
- Mid-range hotels typically offer a variety of amenities, including on-site restaurants, fitness centers, and business centers.
- Budget hotels typically offer basic amenities, such as private bathrooms, air-conditioning, and television.

Hostels:

- Hostels in Ireland typically offer a variety of amenities, such as shared kitchens, lounges, and laundry facilities.
- Many hostels in Ireland also offer Wi-Fi access, as well as continental breakfast.

- Some hostels in Ireland also offer private rooms, as well as dormitory-style rooms.

Guesthouses:

- Guesthouses in Ireland typically offer traditional Irish breakfast.
- Some guesthouses in Ireland also have self-catering facilities.
- Guesthouses in Ireland often have a more homely and intimate atmosphere than hotels.

Vacation Rentals:

- Vacation rentals in Ireland typically offer more space and privacy than traditional hotel accommodations.
- They often have self-catering facilities and they can be found in a variety of locations, such as the countryside, small towns, and cities.
- Some vacation rentals in Ireland also offer additional amenities like a private garden, balcony, or terrace.

When it comes to choosing accommodations in Ireland, it's important to consider the amenities and services that are important to you. Researching the accommodations before booking can help ensure that the accommodation you choose meets your needs and preferences. While luxury hotels offer the most amenities, mid-range hotels and vacation rentals are also a good choice for those who want comfortable accommodations with a variety of amenities. Budget hotels or hostels are a great option for budget-conscious travelers.

Additionally, it's also important to consider the location of the accommodation when choosing where to stay in Ireland. Visitors may want to consider staying in a central location in the city if they plan on exploring the city's sights and culture. For those who prefer a more peaceful and scenic setting, there are plenty of options in the countryside or along the coast.

When it comes to services, luxury hotels in Ireland often offer room service, concierge service, and laundry service. Mid-range hotels and guesthouses generally offer a limited number of services such as front desk service and housekeeping. Budget hotels and hostels typically offer self-service amenities and staff assistance when needed. Vacation rentals often come with a contact person that can be reached for any questions or needs during the stay.

Overall, it's important to research and compare the amenities and services offered by different types of accommodations in Ireland to find the best option for your specific needs and preferences. Whether you're looking for a luxury hotel with all the bells and whistles or a budget-friendly hostel, there is a wide range of accommodations options available in Ireland to suit every taste and budget.

Chapter 3: Transportation

Transportation in Ireland is well-developed, making it easy for visitors to get around and explore the country. Here are the main options for transportation in Ireland:

Public transportation:

- Bus Eireann is the national bus company in Ireland and offers a wide range of services throughout the country.
- Dublin Bus and Bus Éireann are the main bus companies operating in Dublin and they offer a variety of routes throughout the city and its surroundings.
- Irish Rail is the national railway company in Ireland and offers train services throughout the country.
- The Luas is Dublin's light rail system and it offers two lines that connect the city center with the suburbs.

Car rental:

- Car rental is a popular option for visitors to Ireland, as it allows for flexibility and freedom to explore the country at your own pace.
- There are several car rental companies in Ireland, including major international chains and local companies.
- It is important to be aware of the traffic and road conditions, which can be challenging, and to familiarize yourself with the local driving laws and customs.

Taxis:

- Taxis are widely available in Ireland and can be found at taxi ranks or hailed on the street.
- Taxis are metered and fares are regulated by the National Transport Authority.
- There are also a number of app-based taxi services available in Ireland, such as Uber and Free Now.

Driving:

- Ireland has a well-developed road network and traveling by car is a popular option.
- It is important to be aware of the traffic and road conditions, which can be challenging, and to familiarize yourself with the local driving laws and customs.
- A valid driver's license and an International Driving Permit are required to drive in Ireland.

In conclusion, Ireland offers a variety of transportation options to visitors, making it easy to get around and explore the country. Public transportation is widely available and provides convenient and affordable access to major cities and towns. Car rental and taxi services are also popular options, giving visitors the freedom to explore the country at their own pace. Visitors should be aware of the traffic and road conditions and familiarize themselves with the local driving laws and customs before driving in Ireland.

Options for getting around Ireland, including public transportation, taxis, rental cars, and tours

When it comes to getting around Ireland, there are a variety of options to choose from, including public transportation, taxis, rental cars, and tours.

Public Transportation:

- Bus Eireann is the national bus company in Ireland and offers a wide range of services throughout the country.
- Dublin Bus and Bus Éireann are the main bus companies operating in Dublin and they offer a variety of routes throughout the city and its surroundings.

- Irish Rail is the national railway company in Ireland and offers train services throughout the country.
- The Luas is Dublin's light rail system and it offers two lines that connect the city center with the suburbs.

Taxis:

- Taxis are widely available in Ireland and can be found at taxi ranks or hailed on the street.
- Taxis are metered and fares are regulated by the National Transport Authority.
- There are also a number of app-based taxi services available in Ireland, such as Uber and Free Now.

Rental Cars:

- Car rental is a popular option for visitors to Ireland, as it allows for flexibility and freedom to explore the country at your own pace.

- There are several car rental companies in Ireland, including major international chains and local companies.
- It is important to be aware of the traffic and road conditions, which can be challenging, and to familiarize yourself with the local driving laws and customs.

Tours:

- Tour companies in Ireland offer a variety of tours, including bus tours, walking tours, and bike tours.
- Many tour companies also offer specialized tours, such as literary tours, whiskey tours, and food tours.
- A guided tour can be a great way to learn more about the culture, history, and landmarks of Ireland.

When it comes to getting around Ireland, there are plenty of options to choose from. Public transportation is widely available and provides convenient and affordable access to major cities and towns. Taxis and rental cars are also popular options, giving visitors the freedom to explore the country at their own pace. Guided tours are also a great way to learn more about the culture, history, and landmarks of Ireland. It's important to consider your budget, travel style, and the type of experience you want to have when choosing the best option for your trip.

Chapter 4: Food and Drink

Ireland is known for its rich culinary tradition, offering visitors a wide range of delicious food and drink options. From traditional Irish dishes to contemporary cuisine, there is something for everyone to enjoy.

Irish Cuisine:

- Irish cuisine is known for its hearty dishes, such as Irish Stew, made with lamb or mutton, potatoes, onions, and carrots.
- Other traditional Irish dishes include colcannon, made with mashed potatoes and cabbage, and boxty, a type of potato pancake.
- Irish seafood is also a must-try, with dishes such as smoked salmon, oysters, and mussels.
- Irish cuisine is also known for its use of fresh, local ingredients and its emphasis on simplicity.

Pub Food:

- Pubs are a staple of Irish culture, and many offer traditional pub food, such as fish and chips, bangers and mash, and shepherd's pie.
- Many pubs also offer a range of sandwiches and burgers, as well as vegetarian options.

Drink:

- Ireland is known for its strong tradition of brewing and distilling, and visitors should not miss the chance to try some of the country's famous beers and whiskies.
- Guinness, Ireland's most famous beer, is a must-try.
- Irish whiskey is also popular and visitors should consider trying a few different brands to find their favorite.
- Ireland is also known for its ciders and many local cider producers offer tours and tastings.

Farmers Markets:

- Farmers markets are a great way to experience the local food culture and to find fresh produce.
- Visitors can find farmers markets in many cities and towns throughout Ireland, offering a variety of locally grown fruits and vegetables, meats, cheeses, and baked goods.

In conclusion, Ireland is a food lover's paradise, offering a wide range of delicious food and drink options. Visitors should try traditional Irish dishes and seafood, as well as pub food. The country is also known for its strong tradition of brewing and distilling, and visitors should not miss the chance to try some of the country's famous beers and whiskies. Farmer's markets is also a great way to experience the local food culture and to find fresh produce. With a rich culinary tradition, Ireland is sure to satisfy any appetite.

Overview of Ireland cuisine and dining options, including recommended restaurants and local specialties

Ireland is known for its rich culinary tradition, and visitors can experience this through a wide range of dining options. From traditional Irish pubs to contemporary restaurants, there is something for everyone to enjoy.

Traditional Irish Pubs:

- Irish pubs are a staple of Irish culture, and many offer traditional pub food, such as fish and chips, bangers and mash, and shepherd's pie.
- Many pubs also offer a range of sandwiches and burgers, as well as vegetarian options.
- In addition to food, pubs are also known for their warm and welcoming atmosphere, and are a great place to

meet locals and experience Irish culture.

Contemporary Restaurants:

- Ireland's food scene has grown and evolved in recent years, with many contemporary restaurants now available in major cities and towns throughout the country.
- Visitors can find a wide range of cuisines, including Irish, European, Asian and more.
- These restaurants offer a more upscale dining experience, often featuring high-quality ingredients and innovative cooking techniques.

Seafood:

- Ireland is known for its seafood, and visitors should not miss the chance to try some of the country's famous seafood dishes.
- Irish seafood specialties include smoked salmon, oysters, and mussels.

- Visitors can also find a variety of fish and shellfish dishes on restaurant menus.

Farm-to-Table:

- The farm-to-table movement is growing in Ireland and many restaurants now source their ingredients from local farms and producers.
- These restaurants offer a more sustainable and eco-friendly dining experience.
- Visitors can find farm-to-table restaurants in many cities and towns throughout the country.

Specialty Foods:

- Ireland is also known for its specialty foods, such as Irish cheeses, chocolates, and ice cream.
- Visitors can find a wide range of specialty foods in local markets,

specialty food shops, and on restaurant menus.

In conclusion, Ireland offers a wide range of dining options for visitors, from traditional Irish pubs to contemporary restaurants. Visitors should try traditional Irish dishes and seafood, as well as pub food. The country's food scene has grown and evolved in recent years, with many contemporary restaurants now available in major cities and towns throughout the country. The farm-to-table movement is also growing in Ireland and many restaurants now source their ingredients from local farms and producers. Visitors can find a wide range of specialty foods in local markets, specialty food shops, and on restaurant menus. With a rich culinary tradition, Ireland is sure to satisfy any appetite.

Tips on finding the best food and drink experiences, such as local markets, food tours, and cooking classes

When looking for the best food and drink experiences in Ireland, there are several options to consider. From local markets to food tours and cooking classes, visitors can discover the delicious food and drink options that Ireland has to offer.

Local Markets:

- Local markets are a great way to experience the local food culture and to find fresh produce.
- Visitors can find farmers markets in many cities and towns throughout Ireland, offering a variety of locally grown fruits and vegetables, meats, cheeses, and baked goods.
- Visitors can also find specialty food markets, such as seafood markets and cheese markets, which offer a wide

range of locally produced food products.

Food Tours:

- Food tours are a great way to discover the local food culture and to try a variety of different foods and drinks.
- Visitors can find food tours in many cities and towns throughout Ireland, which typically include visits to local markets, restaurants, and food producers.
- Visitors can also find themed food tours, such as seafood tours, whiskey tours, and chocolate tours.

Cooking Classes:

- Cooking classes are a great way to learn about the local food culture and to learn how to make traditional Irish dishes.
- Visitors can find cooking classes in many cities and towns throughout Ireland, which typically include a visit

to a local market, a cooking demonstration, and a meal.

- Visitors can also find specialized cooking classes, such as seafood cooking classes, whiskey and food pairing classes, and chocolate making classes.

Wine and Beer Tasting:

- Ireland is known for its strong tradition of brewing and distilling, and visitors should not miss the chance to try some of the country's famous beers and whiskies.
- Visitors can find beer and whiskey tastings in many cities and towns throughout Ireland, and can also find wine tastings, as well.
- Visitors can also find beer and whiskey tours, which typically include visits to local breweries and distilleries.

In conclusion, Ireland offers a wide range of food and drink experiences for visitors, from local markets to food tours and cooking classes. Local markets are a great way to experience the local food culture and to find fresh produce. Food tours are a great way to discover the local food culture and to try a variety of different foods and drinks. Cooking classes are a great way to learn about the local food culture and to learn how to make traditional Irish dishes. Ireland is known for its strong tradition of brewing and distilling, and visitors should not miss the chance to try some of the country's famous beers and whiskies. Wine and beer tasting are also a great way to experience the local food culture and to find fresh produce. With a rich culinary tradition, Ireland is sure to satisfy any appetite.

Chapter 5: Activities and Attractions

Ireland is a country filled with a wide range of activities and attractions, from natural beauty to historical landmarks, and from outdoor activities to cultural experiences. Visitors to Ireland can explore the country's natural beauty, visit historical landmarks, enjoy outdoor activities, and experience the local culture.

Natural Beauty:

- Ireland is known for its natural beauty, and visitors can experience this through a wide range of activities and attractions.
- Visitors can explore the country's famous landscapes, such as the Cliffs of Moher, Giant's Causeway, and Ring of Kerry.
- Visitors can also enjoy outdoor activities such as hiking, biking, and horseback riding, which offer a great

way to experience the natural beauty of the country.

Historical Landmarks:

- Ireland is home to a wide range of historical landmarks, including castles, monasteries, and ancient ruins.
- Visitors can explore castles such as Dublin Castle, the Rock of Cashel, and Blarney Castle.
- Visitors can also visit monasteries such as Clonmacnoise and Glendalough, and ancient ruins such as Newgrange and Knowth.

Outdoor Activities:

- Ireland is a great destination for outdoor enthusiasts, and visitors can enjoy a wide range of outdoor activities such as hiking, biking, and horseback riding.

- Visitors can also enjoy water sports such as sailing, kayaking, and surfing, as well as fishing and hunting.
- Visitors can also enjoy the country's famous golf courses, such as the Ballybunion Golf Club and the Royal County Down Golf Club.

Cultural Experiences:

- Ireland is known for its rich cultural heritage, and visitors can experience this through a wide range of cultural activities and attractions.
- Visitors can experience the country's traditional music, dance, and theater, and can attend festivals such as the Galway Arts Festival and the Dublin Theatre Festival.
- Visitors can also explore the country's museums, art galleries, and libraries, such as the National Museum of Ireland and the National Library of Ireland.

In conclusion, Ireland offers a wide range of activities and attractions for visitors, from natural beauty to historical landmarks, and from outdoor activities to cultural experiences. Visitors can explore the country's famous landscapes, visit historical landmarks, enjoy outdoor activities, and experience the local culture. Ireland is a great destination for outdoor enthusiasts, and visitors can enjoy a wide range of outdoor activities such as hiking, biking, and horseback riding. Visitors can also experience the country's traditional music, dance, and theater, and can attend festivals such as the Galway Arts Festival and the Dublin Theatre Festival. Visitors can also explore the country's museums, art galleries, and libraries, such as the National Museum of Ireland and the National Library of Ireland. With a rich cultural heritage, Ireland is sure to provide a memorable and enjoyable experience for visitors of all ages and interests.

Overview of the top things to do and see in Ireland, including museums, landmarks, outdoor activities, and cultural experiences

Ireland offers a wide variety of things to do and see, from historical landmarks to natural beauty and cultural experiences. Visitors can explore museums and landmarks, enjoy outdoor activities, and immerse themselves in the local culture. Here are some of the top things to do and see in Ireland:

Historical Landmarks:

- Ireland is home to a wide range of historical landmarks, such as Dublin Castle, the Rock of Cashel, and Blarney Castle.
- Visitors can also visit monasteries such as Clonmacnoise and Glendalough, and ancient ruins such as Newgrange and Knowth.

- Visitors can also visit the famous St. Patrick's Cathedral in Dublin and the Christ Church Cathedral in Cork.

Natural Beauty:

- Ireland is known for its natural beauty, and visitors can experience this through a wide range of activities and attractions.
- Visitors can explore the country's famous landscapes, such as the Cliffs of Moher, Giant's Causeway, and Ring of Kerry.
- Visitors can also enjoy outdoor activities such as hiking, biking, and horseback riding, which offer a great way to experience the natural beauty of the country.

Outdoor Activities:

- Ireland is a great destination for outdoor enthusiasts, and visitors can enjoy a wide range of outdoor activities such as hiking, biking, and horseback riding.

- Visitors can also enjoy water sports such as sailing, kayaking, and surfing, as well as fishing and hunting.
- Visitors can also enjoy the country's famous golf courses, such as the Ballybunion Golf Club and the Royal County Down Golf Club.

Cultural Experiences:

- Ireland is known for its rich cultural heritage, and visitors can experience this through a wide range of cultural activities and attractions.
- Visitors can experience the country's traditional music, dance, and theater, and can attend festivals such as the Galway Arts Festival and the Dublin Theatre Festival.
- Visitors can also explore the country's museums, art galleries, and libraries, such as the National Museum of

Ireland and the National Library of Ireland.

- Visitors can also visit the famous Guinness Storehouse in Dublin, which offers an interactive tour and a chance to learn about the history of Ireland's famous stout.

In conclusion, Ireland offers a wide variety of things to do and see for visitors, from historical landmarks to natural beauty and cultural experiences. Visitors can explore museums and landmarks, enjoy outdoor activities, and immerse themselves in the local culture. Visitors can also visit the famous St. Patrick's Cathedral in Dublin and the Christ Church Cathedral in Cork. Ireland is a great destination for outdoor enthusiasts, and visitors can enjoy a wide range of outdoor activities such as hiking, biking, and horseback riding. Visitors can also experience the country's traditional music, dance, and theater, and can attend festivals such as the Galway Arts Festival and the Dublin Theatre Festival. Visitors can also explore the country's museums, art galleries, and libraries, such as the National Museum of Ireland and the National Library of Ireland. With so much to see and do, Ireland is sure to provide visitors with a memorable and enjoyable experience.

Special events and festivals

Ireland is home to a wide variety of special events and festivals throughout the year, celebrating everything from music and dance to literature and food. Visitors to Ireland can experience the local culture and traditions through these events and festivals, and enjoy a unique and memorable experience.

Music and Dance Festivals:

- Ireland is known for its rich musical heritage, and visitors can experience this through a wide range of music and dance festivals.
- Visitors can attend the Galway Arts Festival, which features a wide range

of music and dance performances from local and international artists.
- Visitors can also attend the Willie Clancy Summer School, which is an annual traditional music and dance festival in County Clare.

Literary Festivals:

- Ireland is home to many literary festivals, celebrating the country's famous authors and poets.
- Visitors can attend the Dublin Writers Festival, which features a wide range of literary events, readings, and workshops.
- Visitors can also attend the Listowel Writers' Week, which is an annual literary festival in County Kerry.

Food Festivals:

- Ireland is home to many food festivals, celebrating the country's delicious cuisine and local produce.

- Visitors can attend the Galway Food Festival, which features a wide range of food and drink events, tastings, and workshops.
- Visitors can also attend the West Cork Food Festival, which is an annual food festival in County Cork.

St. Patrick's Day:

- St. Patrick's Day is one of the most famous festivals in Ireland, celebrated on March 17th, honoring the patron saint of Ireland.
- Visitors can experience St. Patrick's Day Parade in Dublin, which is one of the most famous events in the world, featuring colorful floats and Irish music.
- Visitors can also attend St. Patrick's Day Festival in other cities such as Cork, Galway, and Limerick.

In conclusion, Ireland is home to a wide variety of special events and festivals throughout the year, celebrating everything from music and dance to literature and food. Visitors to Ireland can experience the local culture and traditions through these events and festivals, and enjoy a unique and memorable experience. Visitors can attend the Galway Arts Festival, which features a wide range of music and dance performances from local and international artists. Visitors can also attend the Willie Clancy Summer School, which is an annual traditional music and dance festival in County Clare. Visitors can attend the Dublin Writers Festival, which features a wide range of literary events, readings, and workshops. Visitors can also attend the Listowel Writers' Week, which is an annual literary festival in County Kerry. Visitors can attend the Galway Food Festival, which features a wide range of food and drink events, tastings, and workshops. Visitors can also attend the West Cork Food Festival, which is an annual food festival in County Cork. With a variety of events and festivals to choose from, there is something for everyone to enjoy in Ireland.

Chapter 6: Traveling with kids and families

Traveling with kids and families can be a fun and rewarding experience, but it also requires a bit of planning and preparation. Ireland is a great destination for families, offering a wide range of kid-friendly activities and attractions.

Attractions:

- Ireland is home to many kid-friendly attractions, including the Dublin Zoo, which is home to over 400 animals from all around the world.
- The National Aquatic Centre in Dublin is also a popular attraction for families, offering a wide range of water activities and slides.
- The Cliffs of Moher, one of the most popular tourist destinations in Ireland, is also a great place to visit with kids, offering spectacular views and hiking trails.

- The Viking Triangle in Waterford is another great place to visit with kids, where they can learn about the Viking history of Ireland.

Outdoor Activities:

- Ireland is home to many beautiful parks and gardens, perfect for picnics and family outings. Phoenix Park in Dublin and the Cork City Gaol are great places to spend a day with the kids.
- The Wicklow Mountains offer great opportunities for hiking and outdoor activities with the kids.
- The beaches in Ireland are also great places for kids to play and swim.

Kid-friendly Accommodations:

- Ireland offers a wide range of kid-friendly accommodations, from family-friendly hotels to vacation rentals.

- Some hotels offer special packages and amenities for families, such as children's menus and play areas.
- Vacation rentals are a great option for families, as they offer more space and privacy than a hotel room.

Transportation:

- Ireland has an excellent public transportation system, including buses, trains, and trams, which makes it easy to get around with kids.
- Taxis and rental cars are also available, but it's important to consider the size and the safety features of the vehicle before booking.

Tips for traveling with kids:

- Plan ahead and make sure to bring along all the necessary items such as snacks, medications, and extra clothes.

- Make sure to check the opening hours and prices of the attractions you plan to visit.
- It's important to be flexible and keep an open mind, as things may not always go as planned.
- Lastly, take time to rest and relax, and don't try to cram too many activities into one day.

In conclusion, Ireland is a great destination for families, offering a wide range of kid-friendly activities and attractions. Visitors can experience the Dublin Zoo, National Aquatic Centre, Cliffs of Moher, Viking Triangle, Phoenix Park, Cork City Gaol and the Wicklow Mountains. Ireland offers a wide range of kid-friendly accommodations, from family-friendly hotels to vacation rentals. Ireland has an excellent public transportation system, including buses, trains, and trams, which makes it easy to get around with kids. It's important to plan ahead and be flexible when traveling with kids, and to take time to rest and relax during the trip. With the right planning and preparation, a family trip to Ireland can be a fun and memorable experience for all.

Kid-friendly attractions and activities

Ireland offers a wide range of kid-friendly attractions and activities that are sure to delight and entertain children of all ages. From museums and zoos to outdoor adventures and interactive experiences, there is something for everyone to enjoy.

Museums:

- The National Museum of Ireland in Dublin is a great place to take kids, with interactive exhibits and hands-on activities that make learning fun.
- The Science Gallery Dublin is another great option for families, with interactive exhibits and workshops

that allow kids to explore and experiment.

- The Irish Museum of Modern Art in Dublin is also worth a visit, with exhibitions and activities that encourage kids to explore their creativity.

Zoos and Wildlife:

- Dublin Zoo is one of the most popular attractions for families in Ireland, home to over 400 animals from around the world.
- Fota Wildlife Park in Cork is another great option, with over 85 species of animals, including lions, giraffes, and zebras.
- The Seal Sanctuary in Cork is also worth a visit, where kids can learn about the local seal population and even get a chance to see them up close.

Outdoor Adventures:

- The Wicklow Mountains offer a wide range of outdoor activities for kids, from hiking and rock climbing to biking and horseback riding.
- The Phoenix Park in Dublin is a great place for a family picnic or a bike ride.
- The Cliffs of Moher offer spectacular views and a chance to spot local wildlife, such as puffins and seals.

Interactive Experiences:

- The Viking Triangle in Waterford is a great place for kids to learn about the Viking history of Ireland through interactive exhibits and hands-on activities.
- The Cork City Gaol is another interactive experience that allows kids to learn about the history of Ireland through guided tours and interactive exhibits.
- The National Aquatic Centre in Dublin offers a wide range of water activities

and slides, making it a great option for a fun family day out.

In conclusion, Ireland offers a wide range of kid-friendly attractions and activities that are sure to delight and entertain children of all ages. From museums and zoos to outdoor adventures and interactive experiences, there is something for everyone to enjoy. The National Museum of Ireland, Science Gallery Dublin, Irish Museum of Modern Art, Dublin Zoo, Fota Wildlife Park, Seal Sanctuary, Wicklow Mountains, Phoenix Park, Cliffs of Moher, Viking Triangle, Cork City Gaol and National Aquatic Centre are some of the most popular options for families. Whether you're looking for an educational experience or just a fun day out, Ireland has something to offer every family.

Tips for traveling with children

Traveling with children can be a wonderful experience, but it also requires some planning and preparation. Here are some tips to help make your trip to Ireland with kids as enjoyable as possible:

Pack light: Children tend to get bored easily, so it's best to pack only the essentials and keep the bags light. This will make it easier for them to carry their own bags, and will also make it easier for you to keep an eye on them.

Plan ahead: Before you leave, research kid-friendly activities and attractions in the areas you'll be visiting. This will allow you to make the most of your time and avoid disappointment.

Be flexible: Children can be unpredictable, and plans can change. Be prepared to change your itinerary if necessary, and be open to new experiences.

Bring snacks and entertainment: Pack snacks and small toys or games to keep kids entertained during long car rides or waiting times.

Be mindful of nap times: Children need regular naps, so be sure to plan your itinerary around their nap times.

Be prepared for weather: Ireland's weather can be unpredictable, so be sure to pack appropriate clothing and rain gear.

Be respectful of local customs: Ireland is a conservative country and it's important to be aware of local customs and traditions. Be sure to dress appropriately and be respectful of local culture.

Consider hiring a babysitter: If you want to enjoy a night out without the kids, consider hiring a babysitter or au pair. This will give you the opportunity to relax and enjoy some adult time.

Find family-friendly accommodation: Look for accommodation that caters to families, such as hotels with kids' clubs or vacation rentals with a playground.

Find family-friendly transportation: Look for transportation options that cater to families, such as car rental companies with child seats or buses with play areas.

In conclusion, traveling with children to Ireland can be a wonderful experience, but it also requires some planning and preparation. It is important to plan ahead and research kid-friendly activities and attractions, be flexible, and pack light. Be mindful of nap times, be prepared for weather and be respectful of local customs. Consider hiring a babysitter, find family-friendly accommodation and transportation and make sure to pack snacks and entertainment. With these tips in mind, you can make your trip to Ireland with kids as enjoyable and stress-free as possible.

Chapter 7: Shopping

Shopping in Ireland offers a unique and diverse experience, with a wide range of options for visitors to choose from. From traditional Irish crafts to designer fashion, there is something for everyone to enjoy.

Traditional Irish Crafts:

- The Irish Crafts Council is a great resource for finding high-quality traditional Irish crafts such as Celtic jewelry, woolen sweaters, and traditional pottery.
- The Kilkenny Shop in Dublin is another popular destination for traditional Irish crafts and souvenirs, with a wide range of products including pottery, jewelry, and clothing.
- The Claddagh Gold Factory in Galway is a must-visit destination for traditional Irish jewelry, including the famous Claddagh rings, which

symbolize love, loyalty, and friendship.

Designer Fashion:

- Dublin's Grafton Street is the city's main shopping destination, with high-end brands such as Gucci, Prada, and Louis Vuitton.
- The Powerscourt Townhouse Centre in Dublin is another popular destination for designer fashion, with a wide range of luxury brands and independent boutiques.
- Brown Thomas in Dublin, Cork and Limerick is one of Ireland's most iconic department stores, offering luxury fashion, beauty, and home décor.

Markets:

- The Temple Bar Food Market in Dublin is a great place to find local produce and artisanal food products.

- The English Market in Cork is another popular destination for foodies, with a wide range of local produce and specialty food products.
- The Galway Farmers Market is a great place to find fresh, local produce and other Irish specialties.

Shopping Centers:

- The Dundrum Town Centre in Dublin is one of Ireland's largest shopping centers, with over 150 shops, restaurants, and entertainment options.
- The Kildare Village Designer Outlet is a great destination for bargain shoppers, with discounts on designer fashion and luxury brands.
- The Liffey Valley Shopping Centre in Dublin is a popular destination for those looking for a wide range of shops and services in one location.

In conclusion, Shopping in Ireland offers a unique and diverse experience, with a wide range of options for visitors to choose from. Traditional Irish crafts, Designer Fashion, markets and Shopping Centers are some of the most popular places to shop. The Irish Crafts Council, Kilkenny Shop, Claddagh Gold Factory, Grafton Street, Powerscourt Townhouse Centre, Brown Thomas, Temple Bar Food Market, English Market, Galway Farmers Market, Dundrum Town Centre, Kildare Village Designer Outlet, Liffey Valley Shopping Centre are some of the most popular destinations. Whether you're looking for traditional Irish crafts, designer fashion, or just a unique shopping experience, Ireland has something to offer every shopper.

Chapter 8: Overview of the local shopping scene in Ireland , including markets, boutiques, and souvenir shops

The local shopping scene in Ireland offers a diverse and unique experience for visitors. From traditional markets to high-end boutiques, there is something for everyone to enjoy.

Markets:

- The local markets in Ireland offer a wide range of products, from fresh produce and artisanal food products to traditional crafts and souvenirs. Some of the most popular markets include the Temple Bar Food Market in Dublin, the English Market in Cork, and the Galway Farmers Market. These markets are great places to find unique and authentic Irish products, as well as to experience the local culture and customs.

Boutiques:

- Ireland's boutiques offer a wide range of products, from designer fashion to handmade crafts and souvenirs. Some of the most popular boutiques include the Kilkenny Shop in Dublin, which offers a wide range of traditional Irish crafts and souvenirs, and the Claddagh Gold Factory in Galway, which specializes in traditional Irish jewelry. Boutiques are also a great place to find one-of-a-kind pieces and to support local artisans and designers.

Souvenir shops:

- Ireland's souvenir shops offer a wide range of products, from traditional Irish crafts and souvenirs to more modern items such as clothing and accessories. Some of the most popular souvenir shops include the Celtic Gift Shop in Dublin, which offers a wide range of traditional Irish crafts and souvenirs, and the Irish Gift House in Galway, which specializes in traditional Irish jewelry and other gifts.

Shopping centers:

- Ireland's shopping centers offer a wide range of products, from clothing and accessories to home goods and electronics. Some of the most popular shopping centers include the Dundrum Town Centre in Dublin, which is one of Ireland's largest shopping centers, and the Kildare Village Designer Outlet, which offers discounts on designer fashion and luxury brands.

In conclusion, the local shopping scene in Ireland offers a diverse and unique experience for visitors. From traditional markets to high-end boutiques, there is something for everyone to enjoy. Traditional markets such as the Temple Bar Food Market, the English Market, and the Galway Farmers Market, offer a wide range of products, from fresh produce and artisanal food products to traditional crafts and souvenirs. Boutiques such as the Kilkenny Shop and Claddagh Gold Factory are a great place to find one-of-a-kind pieces and to support local artisans and designers. Souvenir shops such as the Celtic Gift Shop and Irish Gift House offers a wide range of products, from traditional Irish crafts and souvenirs to more modern items such as clothing and accessories. Shopping centers such as Dundrum Town Centre and Kildare Village Designer Outlet offer a wide range of products, from clothing and accessories to home goods and electronics.

Tips on finding the best deals, haggling, and shopping locally

When shopping in Ireland, it's important to keep in mind that haggling is not a common practice in most shops and stores. However, there are some places where haggling is possible, such as at markets or street vendors. It's important to be respectful and polite when haggling, and to have a good understanding of the local currency and prices.

One of the best ways to find deals when shopping in Ireland is to shop locally. This means visiting small, independent shops and businesses instead of large chain stores. These local shops often offer unique and authentic products at more affordable prices than their big-name counterparts. Additionally, supporting local businesses helps to keep the local economy strong and promotes sustainable tourism.

Another way to find deals when shopping in Ireland is to shop during sales and clearance periods. Many shops and stores have regular sales and clearance events, where items are discounted by as much as 50% or more. These sales are often advertised in local newspapers and on social media, so be sure to keep an eye out for them.

When shopping for souvenirs, it's important to be mindful of the quality of the products you are buying. Many souvenirs are made in other countries and may not be authentic. It's always best to purchase souvenirs from reputable shops and vendors, and to do some research on the products you are interested in buying. This way you can be sure that you are getting a quality product that is truly representative of Ireland.

One of the best ways to find deals when shopping in Ireland is to visit local markets, street vendors and garage sales. These places often offer unique and authentic products at more affordable prices than big chain stores. Additionally, supporting local markets and small businesses helps to keep the local economy strong and promotes sustainable tourism.

In conclusion, finding the best deals when shopping in Ireland can be a bit of a challenge, but with a little research and preparation, it's definitely possible. Some tips to keep in mind include shopping locally, shopping during sales and clearance periods, and being mindful of the quality of the products you're buying. Additionally, being open to haggling in certain places, such as markets or street vendors, can help you score some great deals. Remember, it's always best to purchase souvenirs from reputable shops and vendors, and to do some research on the products you are interested in buying. This way you can be sure that you are getting a quality product that is truly representative of Ireland.

Chapter 9: Overview of the local nightlife scene in Ireland, including bars, clubs, and live music venues

Ireland is known for its vibrant and lively nightlife scene, with a wide range of options for visitors to choose from. In the capital city of Dublin, the nightlife scene is particularly diverse, with a wide range of bars, clubs, and live music venues to choose from.

One of the most popular forms of nightlife in Dublin is the traditional Irish pub. These pubs are known for their cozy and welcoming atmosphere, as well as their live music and entertainment. Many of them feature traditional Irish music sessions where visitors can listen to live music and even take part in a sing-along. Some of the most famous pubs in Dublin include The Temple Bar, which is known for its live music, and The Brazen Head, which is the oldest pub in Ireland.

Another popular nightlife option in Dublin is live music. From traditional Irish music to contemporary rock and pop, there are countless venues that offer live music throughout the city. Some of the most famous live music venues in Dublin include The Olympia Theater, which hosts a wide range of performances, and The Roisin Dubh, which is known for its indie and alternative music scene.

For those looking for a more contemporary nightlife experience, Dublin has plenty of trendy bars and clubs. From rooftop bars to underground clubs, there's something for everyone. Some of the most popular bars and clubs in Dublin include The George, which is known for its trendy crowd and lively atmosphere, and The Workman's Club, which is a popular spot for live music.

Aside from Dublin, other major cities in Ireland such as Cork and Galway also have a vibrant nightlife scene. Cork is known for its lively atmosphere and the variety of bars and pubs. The city is also home to several music venues, such as Cyprus Avenue and the Everyman Theatre, which host live music performances regularly. In Galway, visitors can enjoy a wide range of pubs and bars, many of which feature live music performances. The city is also known for its traditional Irish music scene, which can be found in venues such as Taaffes Bar and The Crane Bar.

In conclusion, Ireland has a vibrant and diverse nightlife scene, with something for everyone. Visitors can enjoy traditional Irish pubs, live music venues, trendy bars and clubs, and even gay-friendly bars and clubs. The capital city of Dublin offers the most diverse options, but other major cities such as Cork and Galway also have a lively nightlife scene. It's always a good idea to check online and ask locals for recommendations to make the most of your night out in Ireland.

Chapter 10: Practical Information

When planning a trip to Ireland, it's important to be prepared with practical information to ensure a safe and enjoyable experience. This includes information on local laws and customs, medical facilities, and emergency resources.

First, it's important to be aware of local laws and customs. Ireland has strict laws on drug offenses and drinking and driving, and visitors should be aware of these laws and avoid breaking them. It is also important to be aware of local customs, such as taking off your shoes before entering someone's home.

Next, it's important to know about medical facilities and emergency resources in case of an emergency. Ireland has a well-developed healthcare system, and visitors can find hospitals and clinics throughout the country. It's a good idea to bring your health insurance card with you and to be familiar with the emergency phone number, 112.

When it comes to staying safe, it's important to be aware of your surroundings and take the usual precautions. Be aware of your personal belongings and avoid carrying large amounts of cash or valuables with you. It's also a good idea to carry a photocopy of your passport and other important documents in case they get lost or stolen.

Regarding the Language, English is the most widely spoken language in Ireland, but visitors may also encounter Irish Gaelic, especially in rural areas. It's a good idea to learn a few basic phrases in Irish Gaelic, such as "Dia dhuit" (Hello) and "Slán go fóill" (Goodbye).

Finally, when it comes to currency and payment, the Euro is the official currency of Ireland. Visa and MasterCard are widely accepted, and ATMs are widely available throughout the country. It's a good idea to carry some cash with you, as some smaller establishments may not accept cards.

In conclusion, Ireland is a safe and welcoming country to visit, but it's important to be prepared with practical information to ensure a safe and enjoyable experience. Be aware of local laws and customs, know about medical facilities and emergency resources, stay aware of your surroundings, learn some basic phrases in Irish Gaelic, and familiarize yourself with the currency and payment options.

Tips on staying safe and healthy while traveling in Ireland , including information on local laws and customs, medical facilities, and emergency resources

When traveling to Ireland, it is essential to be aware of the local laws and customs to ensure a safe and enjoyable trip. Ireland has strict laws on drug offenses and drinking and driving, and it is important to abide by these laws to avoid any legal issues. It is also important to note that smoking is prohibited in all enclosed workplaces and public places, including pubs and restaurants.

Another important aspect to consider when traveling to Ireland is the weather. The climate can be unpredictable, and it is essential to be prepared for all weather conditions. It is recommended to bring warm and waterproof clothing, as well as comfortable walking shoes, as the terrain can be uneven.

When it comes to staying healthy while traveling in Ireland, it is important to be aware of the local medical facilities and emergency resources in case of an emergency. Ireland has a well-developed healthcare system, and visitors can find hospitals and clinics throughout the country. It is a good idea to bring your health insurance card with you and to be familiar with the emergency phone number, 112.

It is also important to be mindful of the food and water when traveling in Ireland. It is recommended to stick to well-cooked and hot foods, and to avoid consuming raw or undercooked meats, fish, and eggs. Tap water is safe to drink in Ireland, but it's always a good idea to check with locals if you have any doubts.

When it comes to personal safety, it is essential to be aware of your surroundings and take the usual precautions. Be aware of your personal belongings and avoid carrying large amounts of cash or valuables with you. It is also a good idea to carry a photocopy of your passport and other important documents in case they get lost or stolen.

In conclusion, Ireland is a safe and welcoming country to visit, but it is important to be prepared with practical information to ensure a safe and enjoyable experience. Be aware of local laws and customs, know about medical facilities and emergency resources, stay aware of your surroundings, and familiarize yourself with the food and water safety tips. Keep your valuables and travel documents safe and with you at all times.

Information on visas and travel insurance

When planning a trip to Ireland, it is important to consider the necessary travel documents, such as visas and travel insurance. Both are essential to ensuring a smooth and enjoyable trip.

First, it is important to check if you need a visa to enter Ireland. Citizens of the European Union (EU), European Economic Area (EEA), and Switzerland do not need a visa to enter Ireland. However, citizens of certain other countries may need a visa to enter the country. It is recommended to check the visa requirements for your country of citizenship well in advance of your trip. This can be done by visiting the Irish Naturalization and Immigration

Service website or contacting the Irish embassy or consulate in your country.

Next, it is highly recommended to purchase travel insurance before your trip to Ireland. Travel insurance can provide coverage for unexpected medical expenses, trip cancellations, and lost or stolen personal belongings. There are different types of travel insurance to choose from, such as trip cancellation insurance, medical insurance, and emergency evacuation insurance. It is important to review the coverage and exclusions of the policy you choose and make sure it meets your needs.

When purchasing travel insurance, it is also important to take note of any exclusions or limits on coverage for certain activities such as adventure sports or pre-existing medical conditions. It is also worth checking if your credit card or existing insurance policies, such as home insurance or health insurance, offer coverage for travel.

It is also important to carry a copy of your insurance policy with you at all times, along with contact information for the insurance company's 24-hour emergency assistance line. This will help you to quickly and easily access assistance if needed.

In conclusion, obtaining the necessary visa and purchasing travel insurance are crucial steps in planning a trip to Ireland. It is important to check visa requirements well in advance and to carefully review the coverage and exclusions of any travel insurance policy you purchase. By taking the time to plan and prepare for these practical matters, you can ensure a smooth and enjoyable trip to Ireland.

Tips for a successful and enjoyable trip

When planning a trip to Ireland, there are several tips to keep in mind to ensure that your trip is both successful and enjoyable.

First, it is important to plan ahead and research your destination. This will help you to better understand the local culture, customs, and language, as well as the best times to visit and the top things to see and do. Additionally, researching your destination will help you to plan your itinerary, book accommodations, and make transportation arrangements in advance.

Next, it is important to be prepared for any weather conditions. Ireland's weather can be unpredictable, and it is important to pack accordingly. It is recommended to bring layers of clothing, a waterproof jacket, and comfortable walking shoes. You may also want to pack an umbrella or rain poncho, just in case.

Another important tip is to be mindful of your budget. Ireland can be an expensive destination, and it is important to plan your spending in advance. Consider setting a daily budget and sticking to it as much as possible. Additionally, look for deals and discounts on transportation, accommodations, and activities.

It is also important to be respectful of local customs and culture. Ireland is a very friendly country, and locals are happy to help visitors, but it is important to be mindful of local customs and traditions. For example, it is important to be mindful of the traditional dress code in places of worship, and to be respectful of local customs, such as taking off your shoes before entering a home.

Another tip is to make sure you have a reliable source of information. You can download maps and guides before your trip or carry a guidebook, it will be helpful when you're lost or looking for local recommendations. Also make sure you have a way to communicate with your loved ones back home, either by phone or internet.

Finally, it is important to be open to new experiences and take the time to explore.

Ireland is a beautiful country with a rich culture, and there is so much to see and do. Take the time to explore local markets, try new foods, and visit local landmarks and attractions. It will be a lifetime memory.

In conclusion, by following these tips, you can make the most of your trip to Ireland, and ensure that your trip is both successful and enjoyable. From researching your destination and being prepared for any weather conditions, to being respectful of local customs and culture, and being open to new experiences, these tips will help you to make the most of your time in Ireland.

Dealing with unexpected situations

When traveling, it is important to be prepared for unexpected situations. While it is impossible to predict every possible scenario, there are steps you can take to minimize the impact of unexpected events and ensure that your trip goes as smoothly as possible.

One of the most important things you can do is to have a plan in place in case of an emergency. This includes knowing the location of the nearest embassy or consulate, as well as having contact information for local emergency services and your travel insurance provider. It is also a good idea to carry a photocopy of your passport and other important documents, in case they are lost or stolen.

Another important step is to stay informed about local conditions, such as weather warnings or political instability. This can help you to avoid potential hazards and plan accordingly. Additionally, it is important to stay aware of your surroundings and be mindful of your personal safety, especially when traveling in unfamiliar areas.

When dealing with unexpected situations, it is important to remain calm and think logically. Try to assess the situation and determine the best course of action. If something does go wrong, it is important to have a backup plan in place. For example, if your flight is cancelled, have a plan for how you will get to your destination.

It is also important to be flexible and open to change. Sometimes, unexpected situations can lead to unexpected opportunities, so it is important to be open to new experiences and make the most of your trip.

Another important aspect is to have travel insurance, it can help you to deal with unexpected situations such as medical emergencies, trip cancellations, lost or stolen luggage and more. Be sure to read the policy carefully and understand what is covered and what isn't.

In conclusion, unexpected situations are a part of traveling, and it is important to be prepared for them. By having a plan in place, staying informed, and being flexible and open to change, you can minimize the impact of unexpected events and ensure that your trip goes as smoothly as possible. Remember to always have contact information for local emergency services and your travel insurance provider, also be informed about local conditions and have a good travel insurance policy.

Chapter 11: Itineraries

When planning a trip to Ireland, it is important to have a clear itinerary in order to make the most of your time and see all that the country has to offer. Whether you are a first-time visitor or a returning traveler, there are countless activities and attractions to choose from.

For those with a limited amount of time, a 3-day itinerary in Dublin is an excellent way to experience the city's rich history and culture. Day 1 can be spent exploring the city's historic neighborhoods and landmarks, such as Trinity College and St. Patrick's Cathedral. Day 2 can be dedicated to visiting the city's museums and art galleries, such as the National Museum of Ireland and the Irish Museum of Modern Art. Day 3 can be spent enjoying the city's nightlife and live music scene.

For those with a week or more to explore the country, a road trip around the island is an ideal way to see the diverse landscapes and attractions that Ireland has to offer. Day 1 can be spent in Dublin, Day 2 in the Wicklow Mountains, Day 3 in the Cliffs of Moher, Day 4 in the Ring of Kerry, Day 5 in the Dingle Peninsula, Day 6 in Galway and Day 7 in the Burren.

For those who are interested in history and culture, a visit to the ancient Neolithic tombs at Newgrange, the standing stones of the Hill of Tara and the medieval city of Kilkenny are must-see destinations.

For outdoor enthusiasts, there are countless opportunities for hiking, cycling, and water sports, as well as scenic drives along the Wild Atlantic Way and the Causeway Coastal Route.

For foodies, the country is home to a wide variety of local specialties and world-class restaurants, from traditional Irish pubs serving hearty stew and soda bread to

Michelin-starred restaurants serving modern Irish cuisine.

For families, there are many fun and educational activities to choose from, such as visiting the Dublin Zoo, the Irish National Heritage Park and the Fota Wildlife Park.

Ultimately, the best itinerary for your trip to Ireland will depend on your interests, budget and the amount of time you have available. Whether you are interested in history, culture, outdoor activities, or simply soaking up the local atmosphere, there is something for everyone in this beautiful and dynamic country.

Suggested itineraries for different lengths of stay and interests, including options for solo travelers, families, and couples.

Solo traveler itinerary:

3-day itinerary: Dublin - Explore the city's historic neighborhoods and landmarks, such as Trinity College and St. Patrick's Cathedral, visit the city's museums and art galleries, such as the National Museum of Ireland and the Irish Museum of Modern Art and enjoy the city's nightlife and live music scene.

7-day itinerary: Road Trip - Start in Dublin, move on to the Wicklow Mountains, Cliffs of Moher, Ring of Kerry, Dingle Peninsula, Galway and end in the Burren. This itinerary offers a diverse range of landscapes and attractions that Ireland has to offer and also offers an opportunity for solo traveler to meet other travelers along the way.

Family itinerary:

3-day itinerary: Dublin - Visit the Dublin Zoo, the Irish National Heritage Park and the Fota Wildlife Park. Take a tour of the Guinness Storehouse and Trinity College, and finish the day with a family-friendly show at the Gaiety Theatre.

7-day itinerary: Road trip - Start in Dublin, move on to the Wicklow Mountains, Cliffs of Moher, Ring of Kerry, Dingle Peninsula, Galway and end in the Burren. This itinerary offers a diverse range of landscapes and attractions that Ireland has to offer and also offers an opportunity for families to experience a mix of history, culture and nature.

Couples itinerary:

3-day itinerary: Dublin - Visit Trinity College, St. Patrick's Cathedral and the National Museum of Ireland. Take a romantic stroll through St. Stephen's Green and Phoenix Park. Finish the day with a romantic dinner at a Michelin-starred restaurant.

7-day itinerary: Road trip - Start in Dublin, move on to the Wicklow Mountains, Cliffs of Moher, Ring of Kerry, Dingle Peninsula, Galway and end in the Burren. This itinerary offers a diverse range of landscapes and attractions that Ireland has to offer and also offers an opportunity for couples to experience a mix of history, culture and nature.

It's important to note that these itineraries are just suggestions and can be easily modified to fit your interests, budget, and time constraints. Regardless of your itinerary, Ireland is sure to offer an unforgettable experience.

Final thoughts and next steps

In conclusion, Ireland is a country that offers a wealth of experiences to visitors. From its rich history and culture, to its stunning landscapes and vibrant nightlife, there is something for everyone in Ireland. Whether you are interested in exploring the city or immersing yourself in the countryside, there are countless opportunities for adventure and discovery.

As you plan your visit to Ireland, it's important to consider your interests and budget, and to research the various options available to you. Whether you're looking for budget-friendly accommodations, or looking to splurge on a luxury experience, there are plenty of options available.

When it comes to transportation, you have a variety of options, from public transportation and taxis, to rental cars and tours. Choosing the right mode of transportation will depend on your budget, the length of your stay, and your travel itinerary.

One of the best ways to experience Ireland is through its food and drink. The country's cuisine is known for its delicious and hearty dishes, made with fresh, local ingredients. Whether you're looking to sample traditional Irish fare, or explore the country's burgeoning foodie scene, there are plenty of options available.

When it comes to activities and attractions, Ireland offers something for everyone. From its historic landmarks and museums, to its natural beauty and outdoor activities, there are countless opportunities to explore and discover.

For those traveling with kids and families, Ireland offers a variety of kid-friendly attractions and activities. From zoos and wildlife parks, to family-friendly shows and tours, there are plenty of options to keep the whole family entertained.

Finally, when it comes to shopping, Ireland offers a wide range of options, from local markets and boutiques, to souvenir shops and high-end retailers. Whether you're looking for unique and locally-made souvenirs, or high-end designer fashion, there's something for everyone.

As you prepare for your trip to Ireland, it's important to keep in mind that no matter what you choose to do and see, the country's friendly people and welcoming culture will make your experience even more special. So pack your bags, grab your guidebook and get ready to discover the Emerald Isle.

THE END

Printed in Great Britain
by Amazon

21731337R00068